First published 2023 by Walker Books Ltd,
87 Vauxhall Walk, London, SE11 5HJ

2 4 6 8 10 9 7 5 3 1

© 1985–2023 Shirley Hughes

The moral rights of Shirley Hughes have been asserted in accordance
with the Copyright, Designs and Patents Act 1988

This book has been typeset in Plantin

Printed in China

All rights reserved. No part of this book may be reproduced, transmitted
or stored in an information retrieval system in any form or by any means, graphic,
electronic or mechanical, including photocopying, taping and recording,
without prior written permission from the publisher.

British Library Cataloguing in Publication Data:
a catalogue record for this book is available
from the British Library

ISBN: 978-1-5295-1511-4

www.walker.co.uk

Every effort has been made to trace copyright ownership of the material used herein.
If any omissions have been made, the publisher will be happy to
make any necessary corrections in future printings.

THE SHIRLEY HUGHES TREASURY

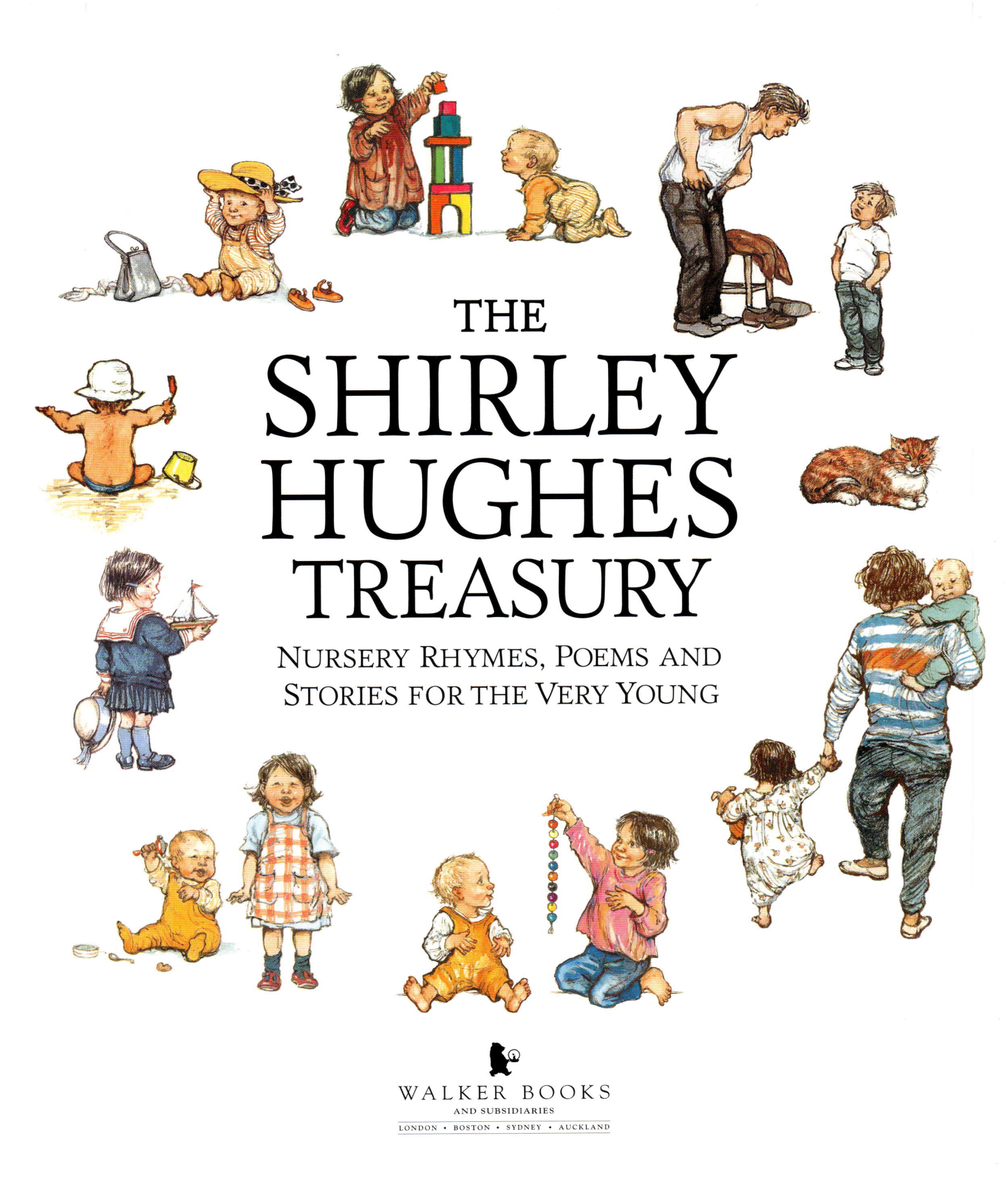

NURSERY RHYMES, POEMS AND
STORIES FOR THE VERY YOUNG

WALKER BOOKS
AND SUBSIDIARIES
LONDON · BOSTON · SYDNEY · AUCKLAND

CONTENTS

Nursery Rhymes

Round and Round the Garden	12
Hot-Cross Buns	12
Humpty Dumpty Sat on a Wall	13
Polly Put the Kettle On	14
Ride a Cock-Horse to Banbury Cross	14
There Was an Old Woman Who Lived in a Shoe	15
Two Little Dicky Birds	16
There's a Worm at the Bottom of the Garden	17
Oh, the Grand Old Duke of York	18
A Sailor Went to Sea, Sea, Sea	19
One, Two, Buckle My Shoe	20
The Queen of Hearts	21
Mary Had a Little Lamb	22
This Little Piggy Went to Market	23
Doctor Foster Went to Glo'ster	23
Incy Wincy Spider	24
Row, Row, Row Your Boat	24
Mary, Mary, Quite Contrary	25
Pat-a-Cake	25
Ring-a-Ring o' Roses	26
One, Two, Three, Four, Five	27
London Bridge Is Falling Down	28
Pussycat, Pussycat	29
Oranges and Lemons	30
Jack and Jill	31
Old MacDonald Had a Farm	32
Five Little Ducks	34
Rub-a-Dub-Dub	36
Five Currant Buns	37
Little Bo-Peep	37
Three Little Kittens	38
Five in the Bed	39
Rain, Rain, Go Away	40
Little Miss Muffet	41
The Man in the Moon	41
Girls and Boys Come Out to Play	42
Diddle, Diddle Dumpling	44
Twinkle, Twinkle, Little Star	44

Poems

Hill	49
Out and About	50
Noisy	52
Spring Greens	54
Squirting Rainbows	56

The Grass House	57
Seaside	58
Sand	59
Splishing and Splashing	60
Water	61
People in the Pond	63
Wet	64
Wind	65
Mudlarks	66
Feasts	67
Misty	68
Fire	70
Fireworks	72
Sick	74
Sunshine at Bedtime	75
Bathwater's Hot	76

Short Stories

Stories Galore	80
Bouncing	82
Old Bones	88
Our Cat Ginger	90
My Friend Betty	91
Hiding	92
Happy Birthday, Dear Mum	96
Giving	98
Chatting	102

Longer Stories

Wheels	108
The Big Concrete Lorry	122

Learning

ABC	136
123	150
Colours	172
All Shapes and Sizes	180

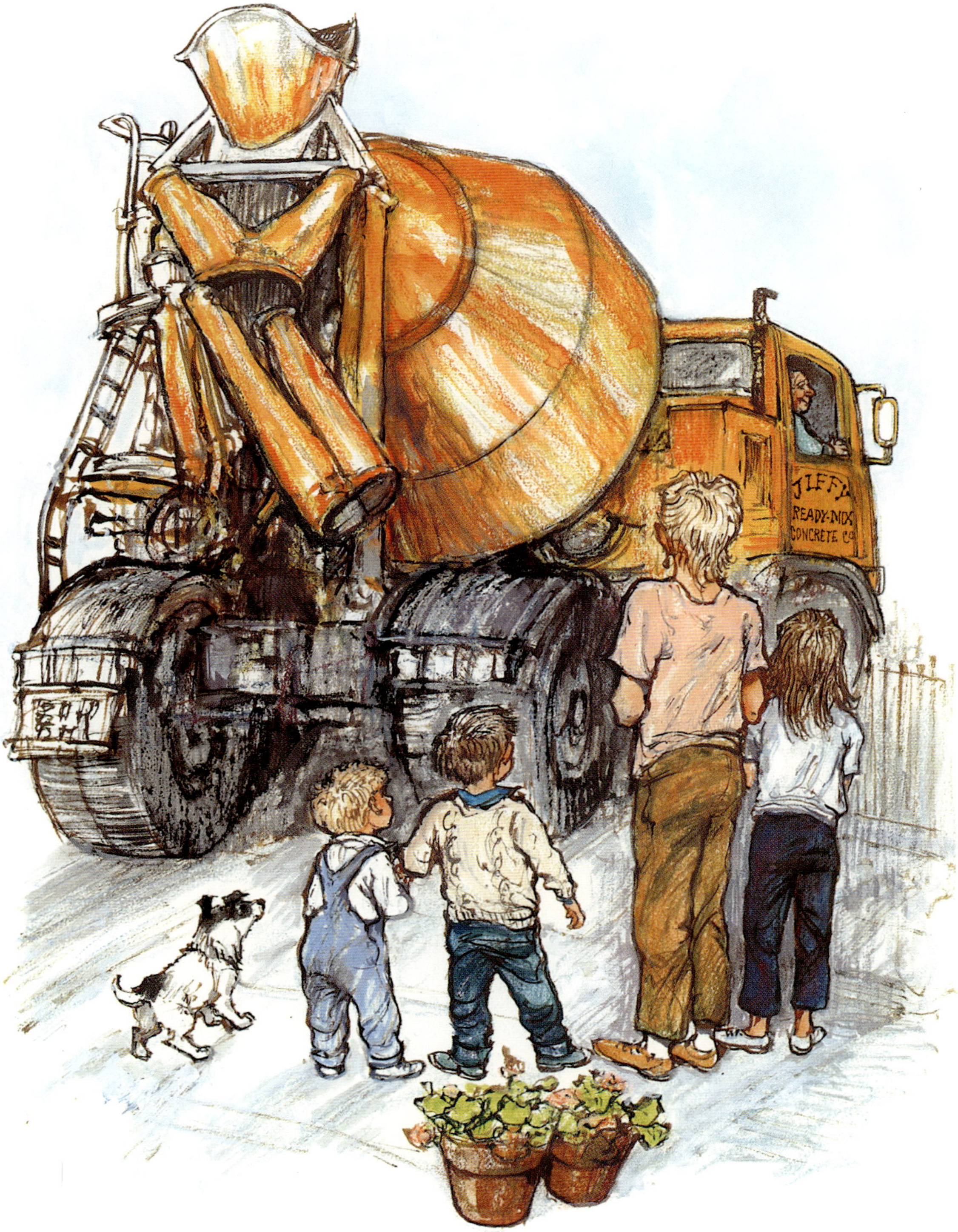
READY-MIX
CONCRETE Co

INTRODUCTION

This book brings together nursery rhymes, poems, stories and learning that celebrate the little and big moments in a child's life.

The collection is divided into five sections that you and your little one can dip in and out of during a quiet time of day, or enjoy together just before bedtime. From traditional rhymes to poems about the magical moments of everyday life, from stories of days out to tales of family and friends, this classic collection from much-loved Shirley Hughes is packed with pages that capture the warmth and fun of her wonderful childhood world.

Nursery Rhymes

Round and Round the Garden

Round and round the garden,
Like a teddy bear.
One step, two step,
Tickle you under there!

Hot-Cross Buns

Hot-cross buns! Hot-cross buns!
One a penny, two a penny,
Hot-cross buns!
If you have no daughters,
Give them to your sons.
One a penny, two a penny,
Hot-cross buns!

Humpty Dumpty Sat on a Wall

Humpty Dumpty sat on a wall,
Humpty Dumpty had a great fall;
All the king's horses
And all the king's men
Couldn't put Humpty together again.

Polly Put the Kettle On

Polly put the kettle on,
Polly put the kettle on,
Polly put the kettle on,
We'll all have tea.

Ride a Cock-Horse to Banbury Cross

Ride a cock-horse to Banbury Cross,
To see a fine lady upon a white horse;
Rings on her fingers and bells on her toes,
And she shall have music wherever she goes.

There Was an Old Woman Who Lived in a Shoe

There was an old woman
Who lived in a shoe.
She had so many children
She didn't know what to do.
She gave them some honey
With butter and bread;
And kissed them all soundly
And put them to bed.

Two Little Dicky Birds

Two little dicky birds
Sitting on a wall.
One named Peter,
The other named Paul.
Fly away Peter,
Fly away Paul,
Come back Peter,
Come back Paul.

There's a Worm at the Bottom of the Garden

There's a worm at the bottom of the garden,
And his name is Wiggly Woo.
There's a worm at the bottom of the garden,
And all that he can do
Is wiggle all night
And wiggle all day
Whatever else the people do say.
There's a worm at the bottom of the garden,
And his name is Wiggly Woo.

Oh, the Grand Old Duke of York

Oh, the grand old Duke of York,
He had ten thousand men,
He marched them up to the top of the hill
And he marched them down again.
And when they were up, they were up,
And when they were down, they were down,
And when they were only half way up
They were neither up nor down.

A Sailor Went to Sea, Sea, Sea

A sailor went to sea, sea, sea,
To see what he could see, see, see.
But all that he could see, see, see,
Was the bottom of the deep blue sea, sea, sea.

One, Two, Buckle My Shoe

One, two, buckle my shoe!
Three, four, knock at the door!
Five, six, pick up sticks;
Seven, eight, lay them straight;
Nine, ten, a big fat hen!

The Queen of Hearts

The Queen of Hearts,
She made some tarts,
All on a summer's day;
The Knave of Hearts,
He stole those tarts,
And took them clean away.
The Queen of Hearts
Called for the tarts,
And beat the knave full sore;
The Knave of Hearts
Brought back the tarts,
And vowed he'd steal no more.

Mary Had a Little Lamb

Mary had a little lamb,
Its fleece was white as snow;
And everywhere that Mary went
The lamb was sure to go.

This Little Piggy Went to Market

This little piggy went to market,
This little piggy stayed at home,
This little piggy had roast beef,
This little piggy had none.
And this little piggy went...
"Wee, wee, wee," all the way home.

Doctor Foster Went to Glo'ster

Doctor Foster went to Glo'ster in a shower of rain.
He stepped in a puddle, right up to his middle,
And never went there again.

Incy Wincy Spider

Incy Wincy spider climbed up the water spout,
Down came the rain and washed the spider out,
Out came the sunshine and dried up all the rain,
And Incy Wincy spider climbed up the spout again.

Row, Row, Row Your Boat

Row, row, row your boat,
Gently down the stream,
Merrily, merrily, merrily, merrily,
Life is but a dream.

Mary, Mary, Quite Contrary

Mary, Mary, quite contrary,
How does your garden grow?
With silver bells and cockle-shells,
And pretty maids all in a row.

Pat-a-Cake

Pat-a-cake, pat-a-cake, baker's man.
Make me a cake as fast as you can.
Pat it and prick it and mark it with B,
And put it in the oven for baby and me.

Ring-a-Ring o' Roses

Ring-a-ring o' roses,
A pocket full of posies,
A-tishoo! A-tishoo!
We all fall down!

One, Two, Three, Four, Five

One, two, three, four, five,
Once I caught a fish alive,
Six, seven, eight, nine, ten,
Then I let it go again.
Why did you let it go?
Because it bit my finger so.
Which finger did it bite?
This little finger on the right.

London Bridge Is Falling Down

London Bridge is falling down,
Falling down, falling down.
London Bridge is falling down,
My fair lady.

Pussycat, Pussycat

"Pussycat, pussycat, where have you been?"
"I've been up to London to visit the Queen."
"Pussycat, pussycat, what did you do there?"
"I frightened a little mouse under her chair.
MEOW!"

Oranges and Lemons

"Oranges and lemons,"
Say the bells of Saint Clement's.
"You owe me five farthings,"
Say the bells of Saint Martin's.
"When will you pay me?"
Say the bells of Old Bailey.
"When I grow rich,"
Say the bells of Shoreditch.
"When will that be?"
Say the bells of Stepney.
"I do not know,"
Say the great bells of Bow.

Jack and Jill

Jack and Jill went up the hill
To fetch a pail of water.
Jack fell down and broke his crown,
And Jill came tumbling after.
Up Jack got, and home did trot,
As fast as he could caper,
He went to bed to mend his head,
With vinegar and brown paper.

Old MacDonald Had a Farm

Old MacDonald had a farm,
Ee-eye, ee-eye-oh!
And on that farm he had a duck,
Ee-eye, ee-eye-oh!
With a "quack, quack" here,
And a "quack, quack" there,
Here a "quack," there a "quack,"
Everywhere a "quack, quack!"
Old MacDonald had a farm,
Ee-eye, ee-eye-oh!

Old MacDonald had a farm,
Ee-eye, ee-eye-oh!
And on that farm he had a dog,
Ee-eye, ee-eye-oh!
With a "woof, woof" here,
And a "woof, woof" there,
Here a "woof," there a "woof,"
Everywhere a "woof, woof!"
Old MacDonald had a farm,
Ee-eye, ee-eye-oh!

Old MacDonald had a farm,
Ee-eye, ee-eye-oh!
And on that farm he had a pig,
Ee-eye, ee-eye-oh!
With an "oink, oink" here,
And an "oink, oink" there,
Here an "oink," there an "oink,"
Everywhere an "oink, oink!"
Old MacDonald had a farm,
Ee-eye, ee-eye-oh!

Five Little Ducks

Five little ducks went swimming one day,
Over the hill and far away.
Mother duck said, "Quack, quack, quack, quack!"
And only four little ducks came back.

Four little ducks went swimming one day,
Over the hill and far away.
Mother duck said, "Quack, quack, quack, quack!"
And only three little ducks came back.

Three little ducks went swimming one day,
Over the hill and far away.
Mother duck said, "Quack, quack, quack, quack!"
And only two little ducks came back.

Two little ducks went swimming one day,
Over the hill and far away.
Mother duck said, "Quack, quack, quack, quack!"
And only one little duck came back.

One little duck went swimming one day,
Over the hill and far away.
Mother duck said, "Quack, quack, quack, quack!"
And all her five little ducks came back.

Rub-a-Dub-Dub

Rub-a-dub-dub,
Three men in a tub,
And who do you think they be?
The butcher, the baker, the candlestick maker,
And all of them gone to sea.

Five Currant Buns

Five currant buns in a baker's shop,
Big and round with a cherry on the top.
Along came a boy with a penny one day,
Bought a currant bun and took it away.

Little Bo-Peep

Little Bo-Peep has lost her sheep,
And can't tell where to find them;
Leave them alone, and they'll come home,
Wagging their tails behind them.

Three Little Kittens

Three little kittens, they lost their mittens,
And they began to cry,
"Oh, mother dear, we sadly fear,
That we have lost our mittens."
"What! Lost your mittens, you naughty kittens!
Then you shall have no pie."
"Meow, meow, meow."
"Then you shall have no pie."

Three little kittens, they found their mittens,
And they began to cry,
"Oh, mother dear, see here, see here,
For we have found our mittens."
"Put on your mittens, you silly kittens,
And you shall have some pie."
"Purr, purr, purr,
Oh, let us have some pie."

Five in the Bed

There were five in the bed and the little one said,
"Roll over, roll over!"
So they all rolled over and one fell out.

There were four in the bed and the little one said,
"Roll over, roll over!"
So they all rolled over and one fell out.

There were three in the bed and the little one said,
"Roll over, roll over!"
So they all rolled over and one fell out.

There were two in the bed and the little one said,
"Roll over, roll over!"
So they all rolled over and one fell out.

There was one in the bed and the little one said,
"Good night!"

Rain, Rain, Go Away

Rain, rain, go away,
Come again another day.
Rain, rain, go away,
Little Katie wants to play.

Little Miss Muffet

Little Miss Muffet
Sat on a tuffet,
Eating her curds and whey;
Along came a spider,
Who sat down beside her,
And frightened Miss Muffet away.

The Man in the Moon

The man in the moon,
Came tumbling down,
And asked his way to Norwich,
He went by the south,
And burnt his mouth
With supping cold pease-porridge.

Girls and Boys Come Out to Play

Girls and boys come out to play,
The moon doth shine as bright as day;
Leave your supper, and leave your sleep,
And come with your playfellows into the street.

Come with a whoop, come with a call,
Come with a good will or not at all.
Up the ladder and down the wall,
A halfpenny roll will serve us all.

Diddle, Diddle Dumpling

Diddle, diddle dumpling, my son John,
Went to bed with his trousers on.
One shoe off and the other shoe on,
Diddle, diddle dumpling, my son John.

Twinkle, Twinkle, Little Star

Twinkle, twinkle, little star,
How I wonder what you are!
Up above the world so high,
Like a diamond in the sky.
Twinkle, twinkle, little star,
How I wonder what you are!

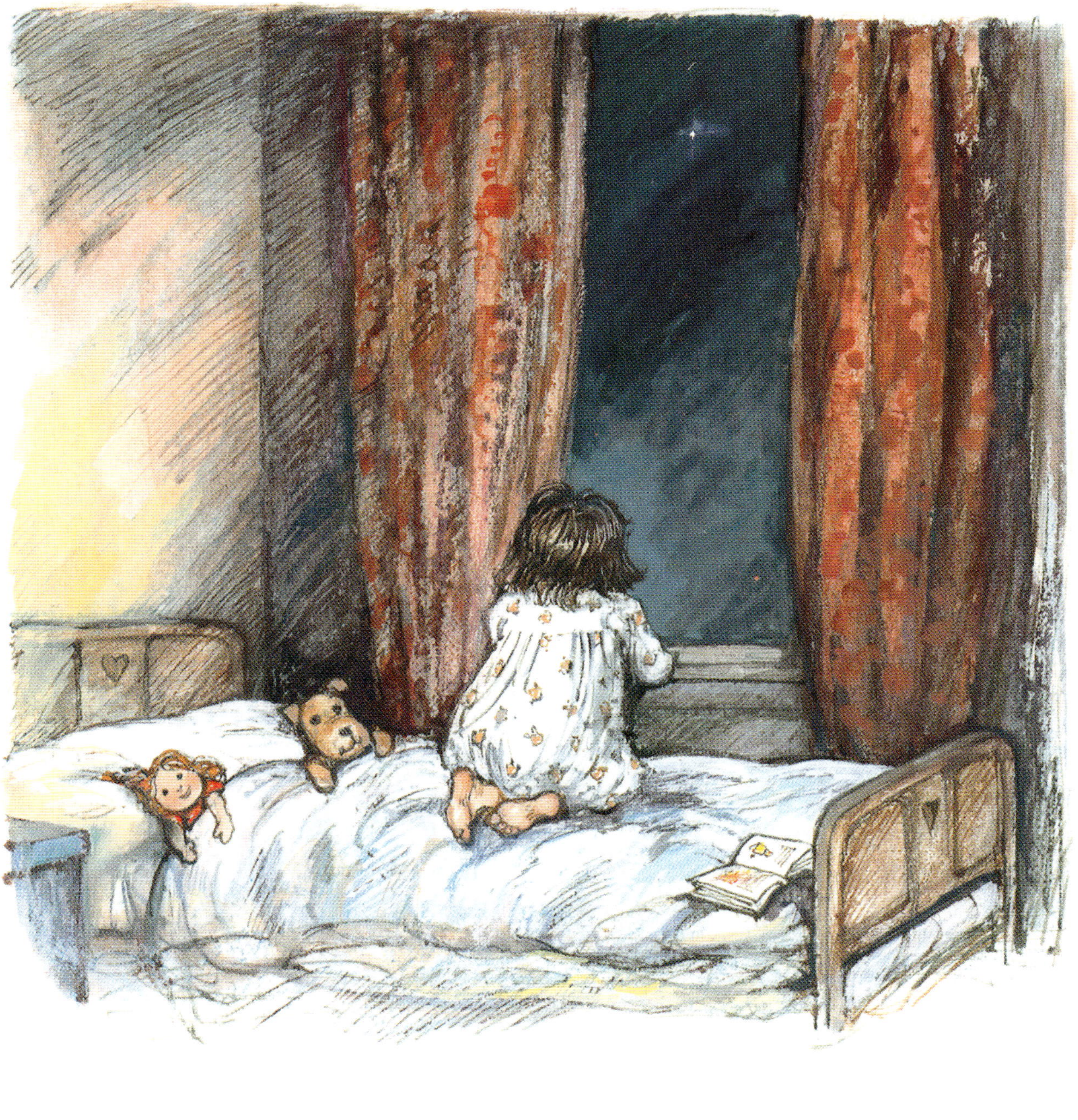

POEMS

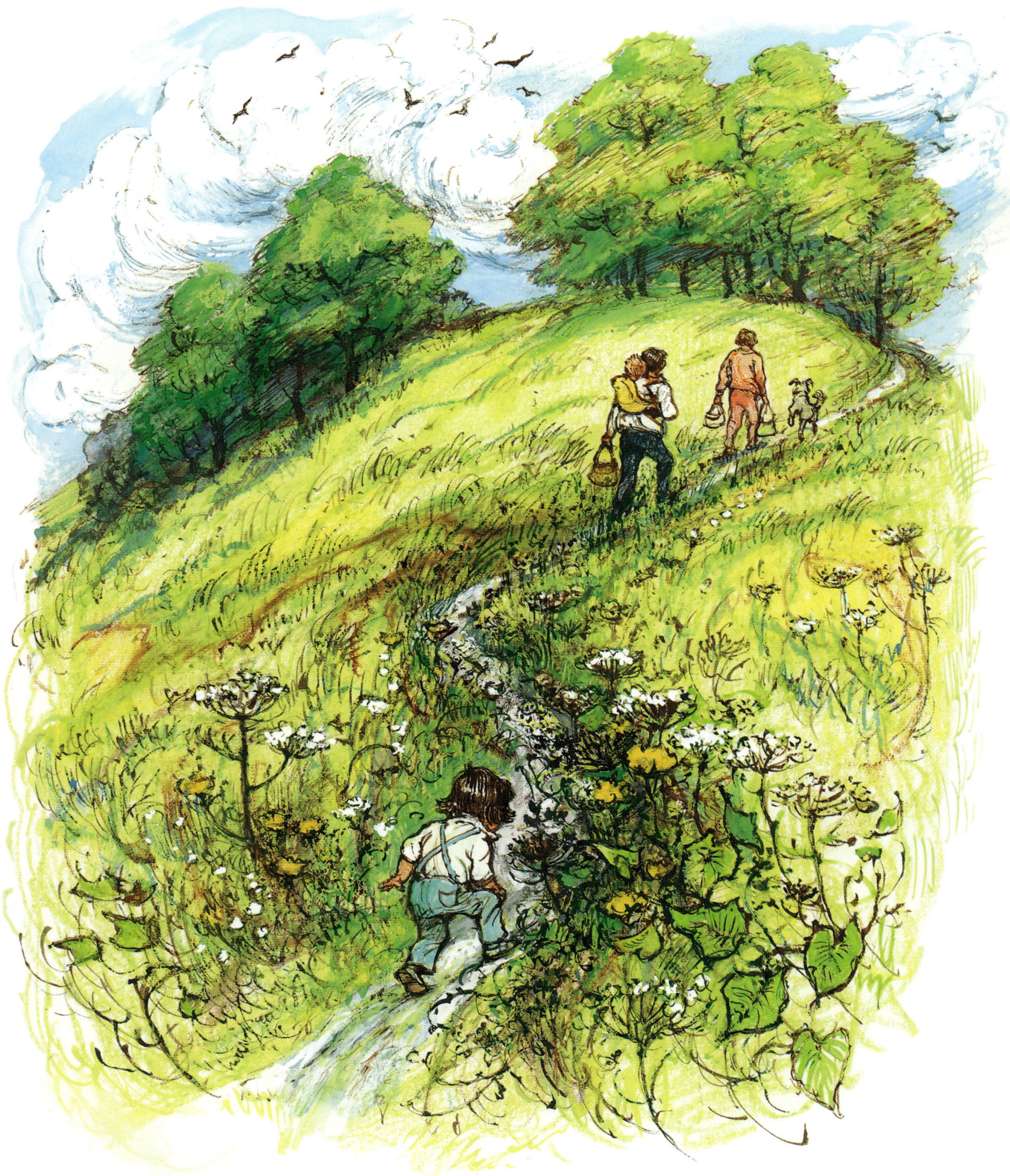

Hill

Huge clouds
Slowly pass;
Huge hill
Made of grass.
Jungle under,
Thick and green,
Tangled stalks –
Creep between;
Scramble up,
Hug the ground…

Suddenly see
All around!
Watch out, fences,
Fields and town!
From the top of the world
I come rolling down.

Out and About

Shiny boots,
Brand new,
Pale shoots
Poking through.
In the garden,
Out and about,
Run down the path,
Scamper and shout.
Wild white washing
Waves at the sky,
The birds are busy
And so am I.

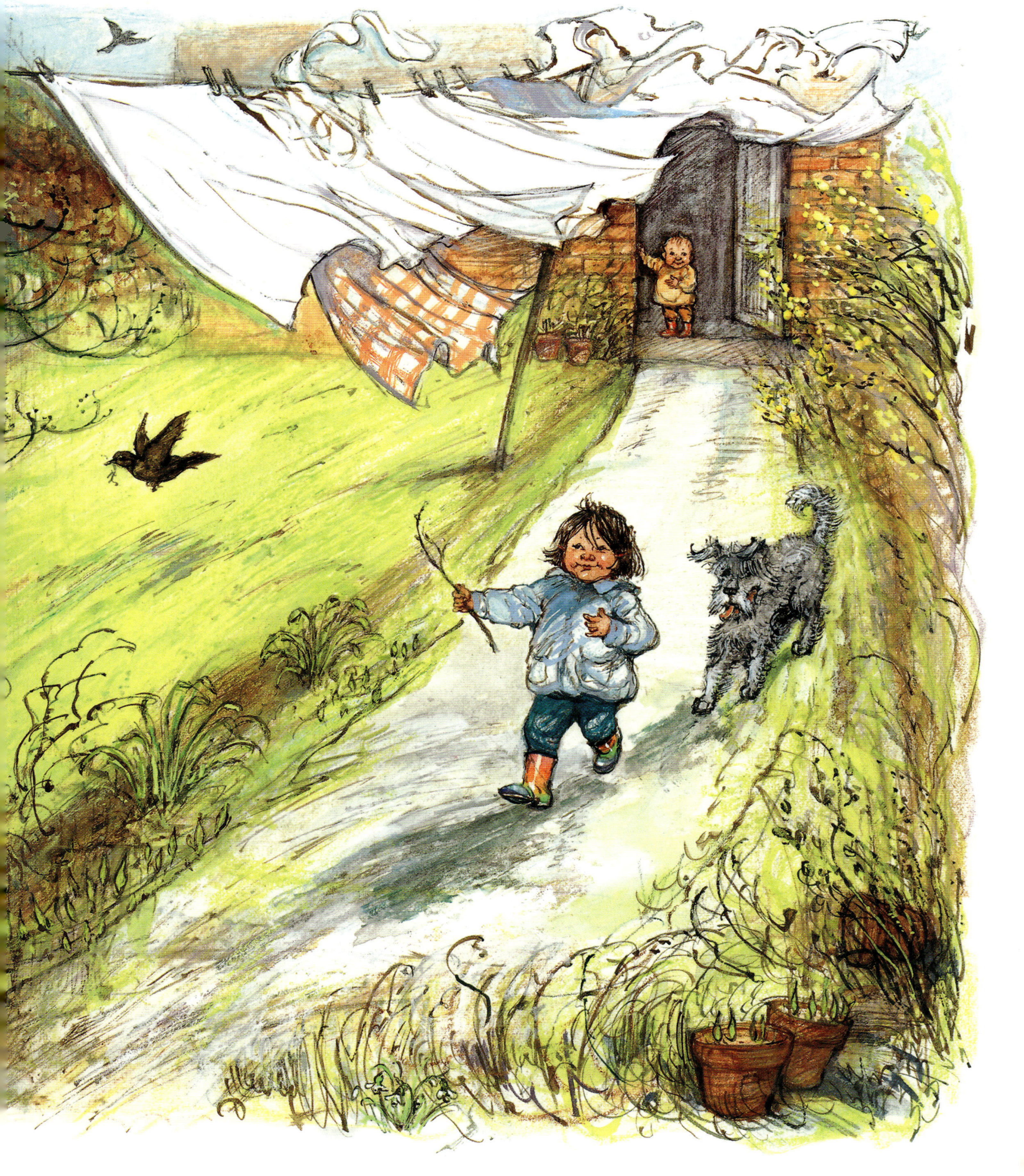

Noisy

Noisy noises! Pan lids clashing,
Dog barking, plate smashing;
Telephone ringing, baby bawling,
Midnight cats cat-a-wauling.
Door slamming, aeroplane zooming,
Vacuum cleaner vroom-vroom-vrooming;
And if I dance and sing a tune,
Baby joins in with a saucepan and spoon.

Gentle noises: dry leaves swishing,
Falling rain, splashing, splishing;
Rustling trees, hardly stirring,
Lazy cat softly purring

Story's over, bedtime's come,
Crooning baby sucks his thumb.
All quiet, not a peep –
Everyone is fast asleep.

Spring Greens

Bulbs in pots,

Twigs in jars,

Dads in the street, washing cars.

Greens in season,

Trees in bud,

Sky in puddles,

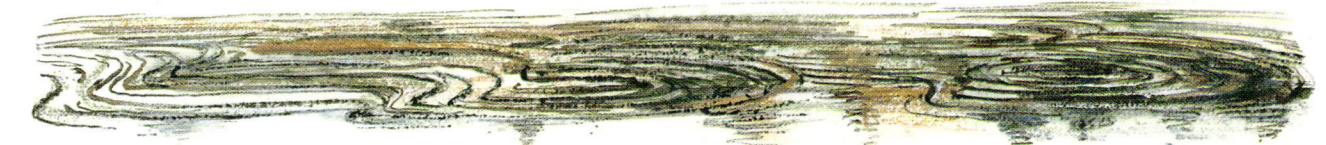

Ripples in mud.

Birds in bushes, singing loud,

Sun tucked up in a bed of cloud.

Squirting Rainbows

Bare legs,
Bare toes,
Paddling pool,
Garden hose.
Daisies sprinkled
In the grass,
Dandelions
Bold as brass.
Squirting rainbows,
Sunbeam flashes,
Backyards full
Of shrieks and splashes!

The Grass House

The grass house
Is my private place.
Nobody can see me
In the grass house.
Feathery plumes
Meet over my head.
Down here,
In the green, there are:
Seeds
Weeds
Stalks
Pods
And tiny little flowers.

Only the cat
And some busy, hurrying ants
Know where my grass house is.

Seaside

Sand in the sandwiches,
Sand in the tea,
Flat, wet sand running
Down to the sea.
Pools full of seaweed,
Shells and stones,
Damp bathing suits
And ice-cream cones.
Waves pouring in
To a sand-castle moat.
Mend the defences!
Now we're afloat!
Water's for splashing,
Sand is for play,
A day by the sea
Is the best kind of day.

Sand

I like sand.
The run-between-your-fingers kind,
The build-it-into-castles kind.
Mountains of sand meeting the sky,
Flat sand, going on for ever,
I *do* like sand.

Splishing and Splashing

Deep in the green shade
Two mums sit, lazily chatting.

But Norah and Katie are busy,
Turning the tap,
Filling buckets
And the watering can,
Slooshing in it;
Making mud,
Making rivers and dams
And swimming pools for ants.

Olly's busy too,
Sitting in a basin of water,
Bailing out.

Water

I like water.
The shallow, splashy, paddly kind,
The hold-on-tight-it's-deep kind.
Splosh it out of buckets,
Spray it all around.
I *do* like water.

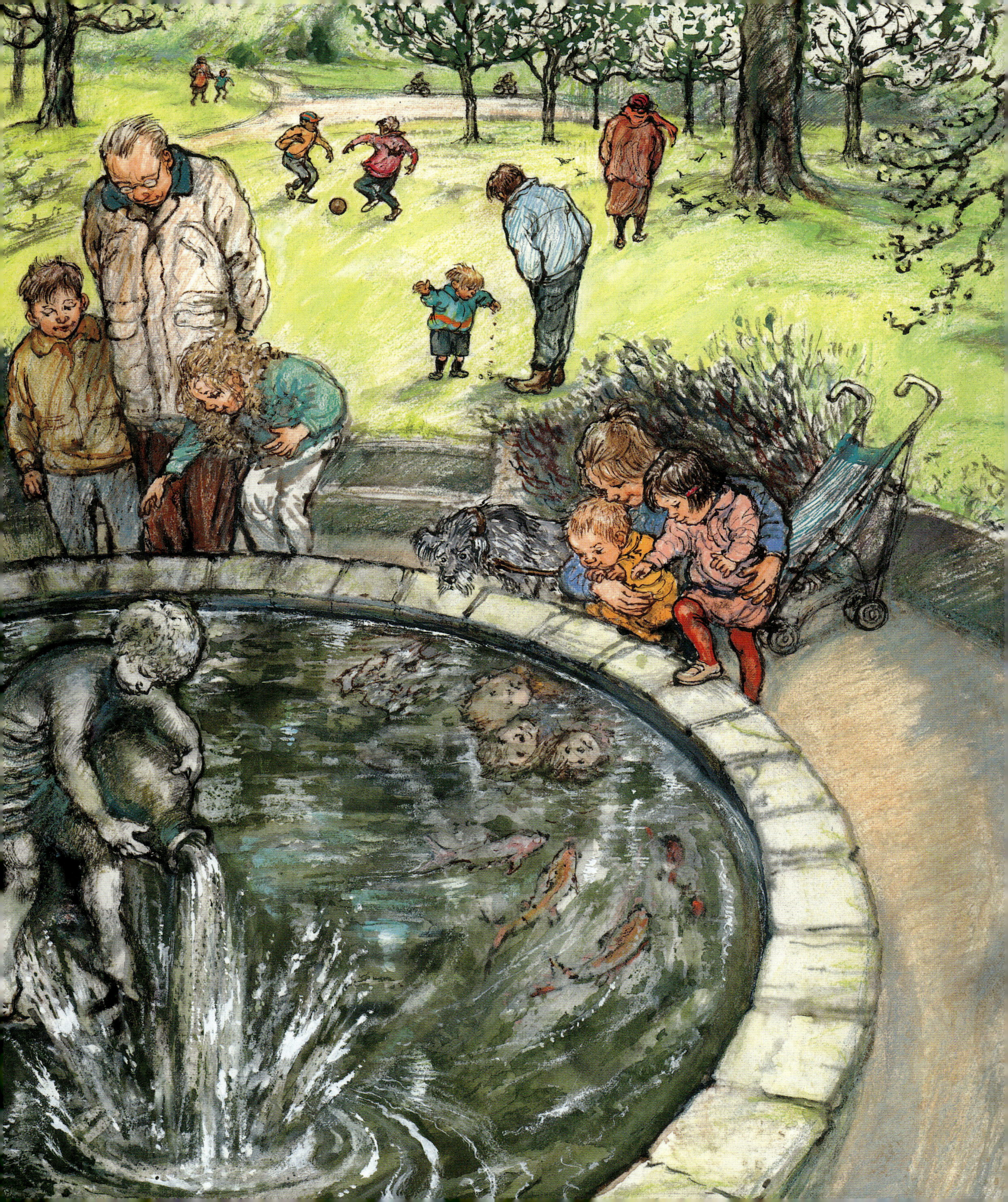

People in the Pond

Peering over the stone rim,
Olly and Katie see four faces
looking back at them:
Buster, Mum, Olly and Katie,
wobbly and green in the water.
Down below, the fish glide,
grey and silver,
pink and gold;
hovering, rising,
then suddenly diving,
with a brisk whisk of their tails,
while the little fish slip in and out like ripples.
Now their faces break up into bits of watery light.
But the boy in the middle of the pond
stands still as stone, endlessly pouring
water from his stone jar.

Wet

Dark clouds,
Rain again,
Rivers on the
Misted pane.
Wet umbrellas
In the street,
Running noses,
Damp feet.

Wind

I like the wind.

The soft, summery, gentle kind,

The gusty blustery, fierce kind.

Ballooning out the curtains,

Blowing things about,

Wild and wilful everywhere.

I *do* like the wind.

Mudlarks

I like mud.
The slippy, sloppy, squelchy kind,
The slap-it-into-pies-kind.
Stir it up in puddles,
Slither and slide
I *do* like mud.

Feasts

Apples heaped on market barrows,
Juicy plums and stripy marrows.
Grains of barley,
Carefully stored,
Feasts of berries,
Nuts to hoard,
And ripe pumpkins, yellow and green,
To light with candles at Hallowe'en.

Misty

Mist in the morning,
Raw and nippy,
Leaves on the pavement,
Wet and slippy.
Sun on fire
Behind the trees,
Muddy boots,
Muddy knees.

Shop windows,
Lighted early,
Soaking grass,
Dewy, pearly.
Red, lemon,
Orange and brown,
Silently, softly,
The leaves float down.

Fire

Fire is a dragon
(Better beware),
Dangerous and beautiful
(Better take care).
Puffing out smoke
As soon as it's lit,
Licking up leaves,
Crackle and spit!

Sending up sparks
Into the sky
That hover a moment
And suddenly die.
Fire is a dragon,
Alive in the night;
Fiery dragon,
Glittering bright.

Fireworks

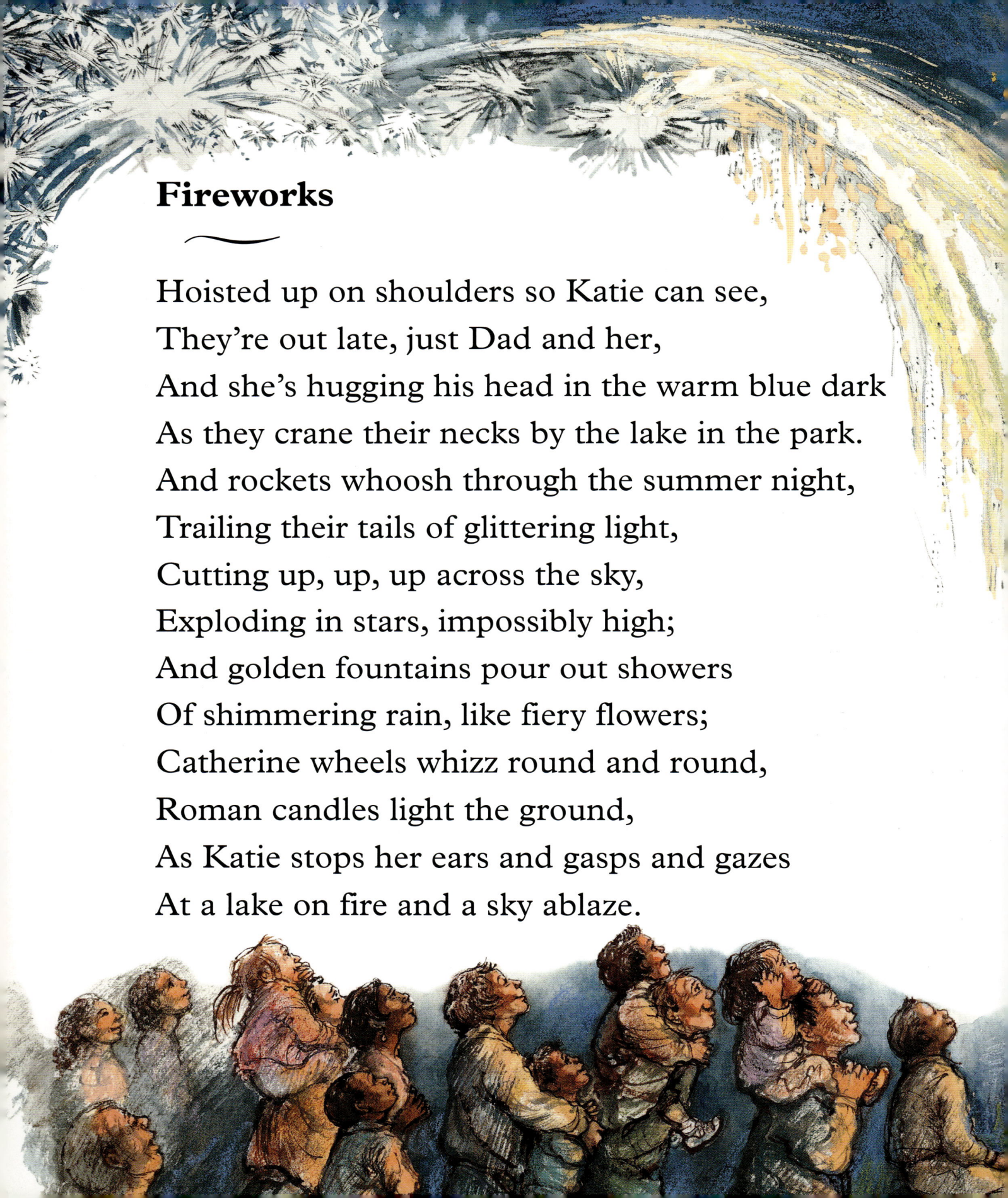

Hoisted up on shoulders so Katie can see,
They're out late, just Dad and her,
And she's hugging his head in the warm blue dark
As they crane their necks by the lake in the park.
And rockets whoosh through the summer night,
Trailing their tails of glittering light,
Cutting up, up, up across the sky,
Exploding in stars, impossibly high;
And golden fountains pour out showers
Of shimmering rain, like fiery flowers;
Catherine wheels whizz round and round,
Roman candles light the ground,
As Katie stops her ears and gasps and gazes
At a lake on fire and a sky ablaze.

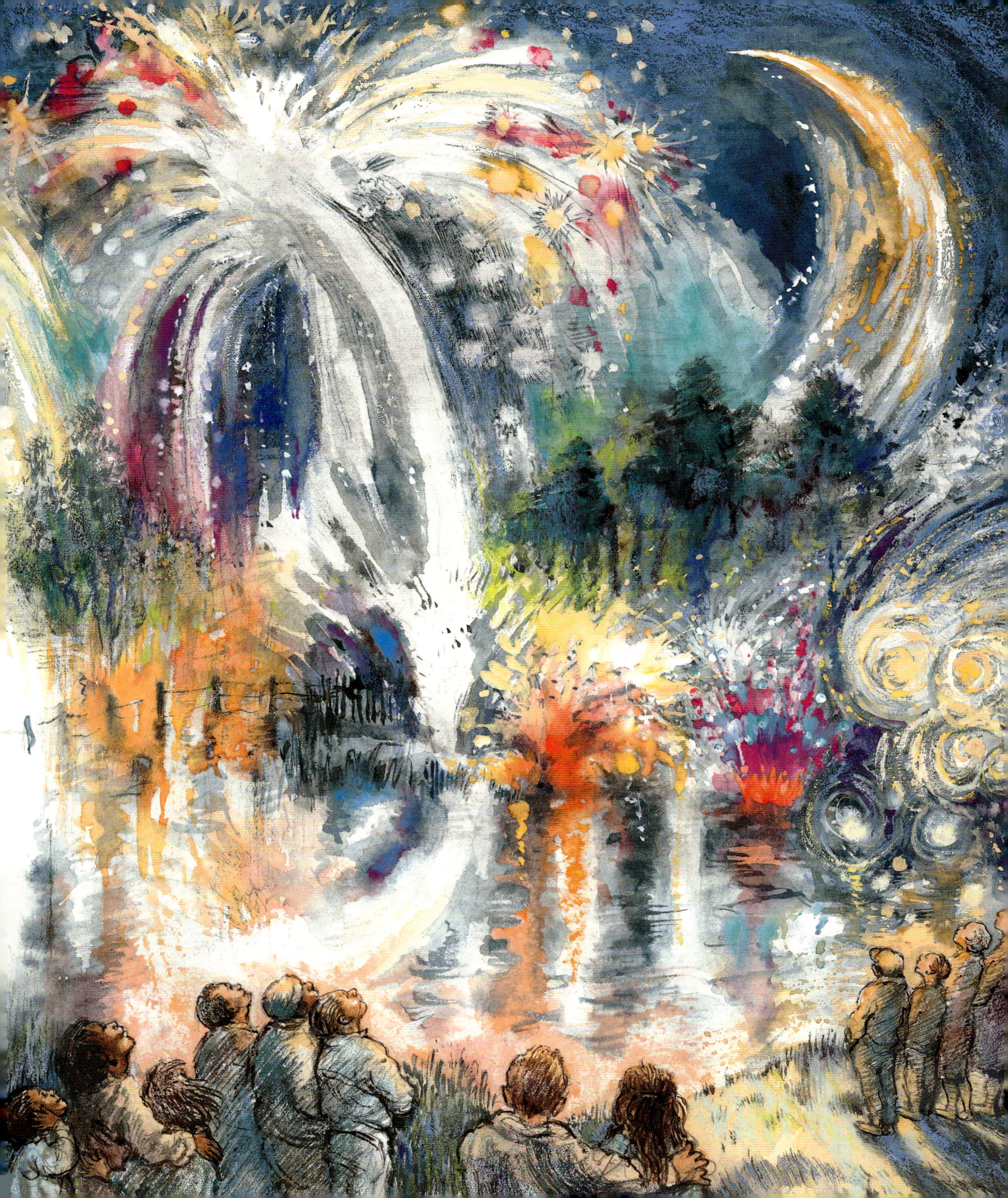

Sick

Hot, cross, aching head,
Prickly, tickly, itchy bed.
Piles of books and toys and puzzles
Heavy on my feet,
Pillows thrown all anyhow,
Wrinkles in the sheet.
Sick of medicine, lemonade,
Soup spooned from a cup.
When will I be *better*?
When can I *get up*?

Sunshine at Bedtime

Streets full of blossom,
Like pink and white snow,
Beds full of tulips,
Tucked up in a row.

Trees full of "candles"
Alight in the park,
Sunshine at bedtime,
Why isn't it dark?

Yet high in the sky
I see the moon,
Pale as a ghost
In the afternoon.

Bathwater's hot

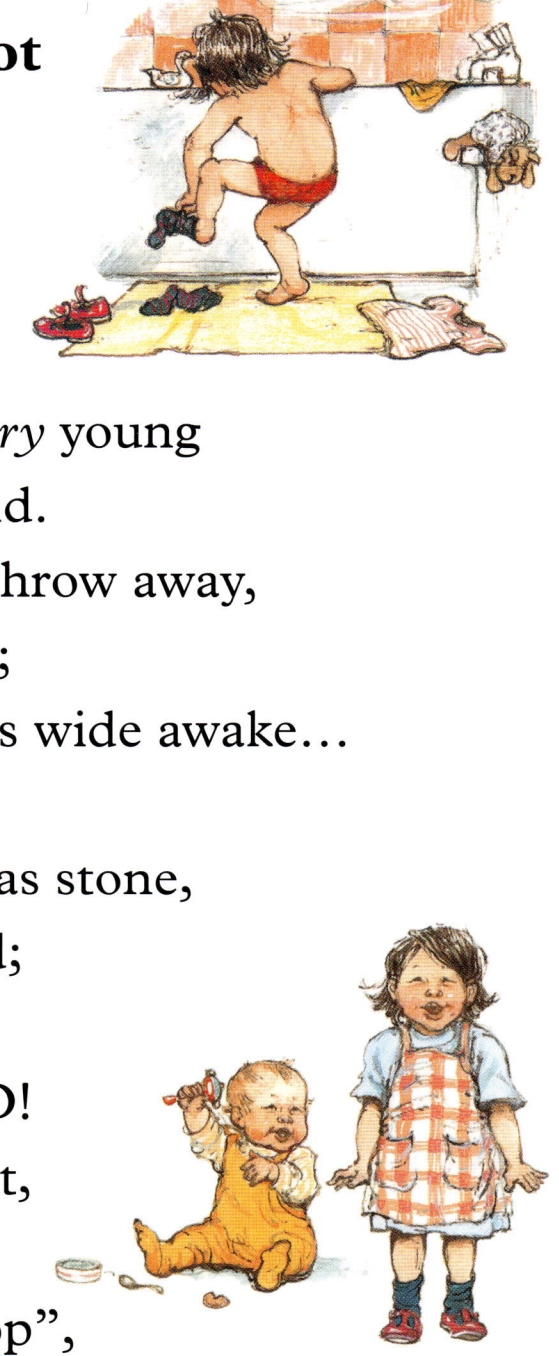

Bathwater's hot,
Seawater's cold;
Ginger's kittens are *very* young
But Buster's getting old.
Some things you can throw away,
Some are nice to keep;
Here's someone who is wide awake…
Shhh, he's fast asleep!
Some things are hard as stone,
Some are soft as cloud;
Whisper very quietly,
SHOUT OUT LOUD!
It's fun to run very fast,
Or to be slow;
The red light says "stop",
And the green light says "go".

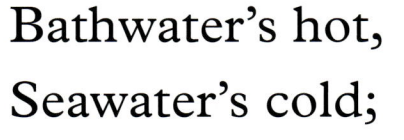

It's kind to be helpful,
Unkind to tease;
Rather rude to push and grab,
Polite to say "please".
Night time is dark,
Day time is light;
The sun says "good morning",
And the moon says "good night".

SHORT STORIES

Stories Galore

Olly and Katie have lots of books. Olly likes chewing his, but he stops doing it when Katie shows him the pictures. Down at the library there are stories galore. Olly and Katie go there on Saturday afternoons. While Mum is choosing her book, Dad and Olly and Katie sit on cushions on the floor while a lady tells them all about the

Three Little Pigs and the Owl and the Pussycat and the Billy Goats Gruff. And Olly sits still and listens without wriggling (well, most of the time, anyway).

When it's time for Katie to choose her books to take home, Dad says: "Why do you always choose the same ones?" And Katie says it's because she likes them best, of course.
But one day, Katie will read
all the books in the library!

Bouncing

When I throw my big shiny ball it bounces away from me. Bounce, bounce, bounce, bounce! Then it rolls along the ground, then it stops.

I like bouncing too.

In the mornings I bounce on my bed, and the baby bounces in his cot. Mum and Dad's big bed is an even better place to bounce. But Dad doesn't much like being bounced on in the early morning.

So we roll on the floor instead, and the baby bounces on ME!

After breakfast he does some dancing in his baby-bouncer, and I do some dancing to the radio.

At my play-group there are big cushions on the floor where lots of children can bounce together.

And at home there's a big sofa where we can bounce when Mum isn't looking. Grandpa and I know a good bouncing game. I ride on his knees and we sing:

This is the way the ladies ride:
trit-trot, trit-trot;
This is the way the gentlemen ride:
tarran, tarran;
This is the way the farmers ride:
clip-clop, clip-clop;
This is the way the jockeys ride:
gallopy, gallopy …

and FALL OFF!

I like bouncing. I bounce about all day ... bounce, bounce, bounce, bounce! Until in the end I stop bouncing, and go off to sleep.

Old Bones

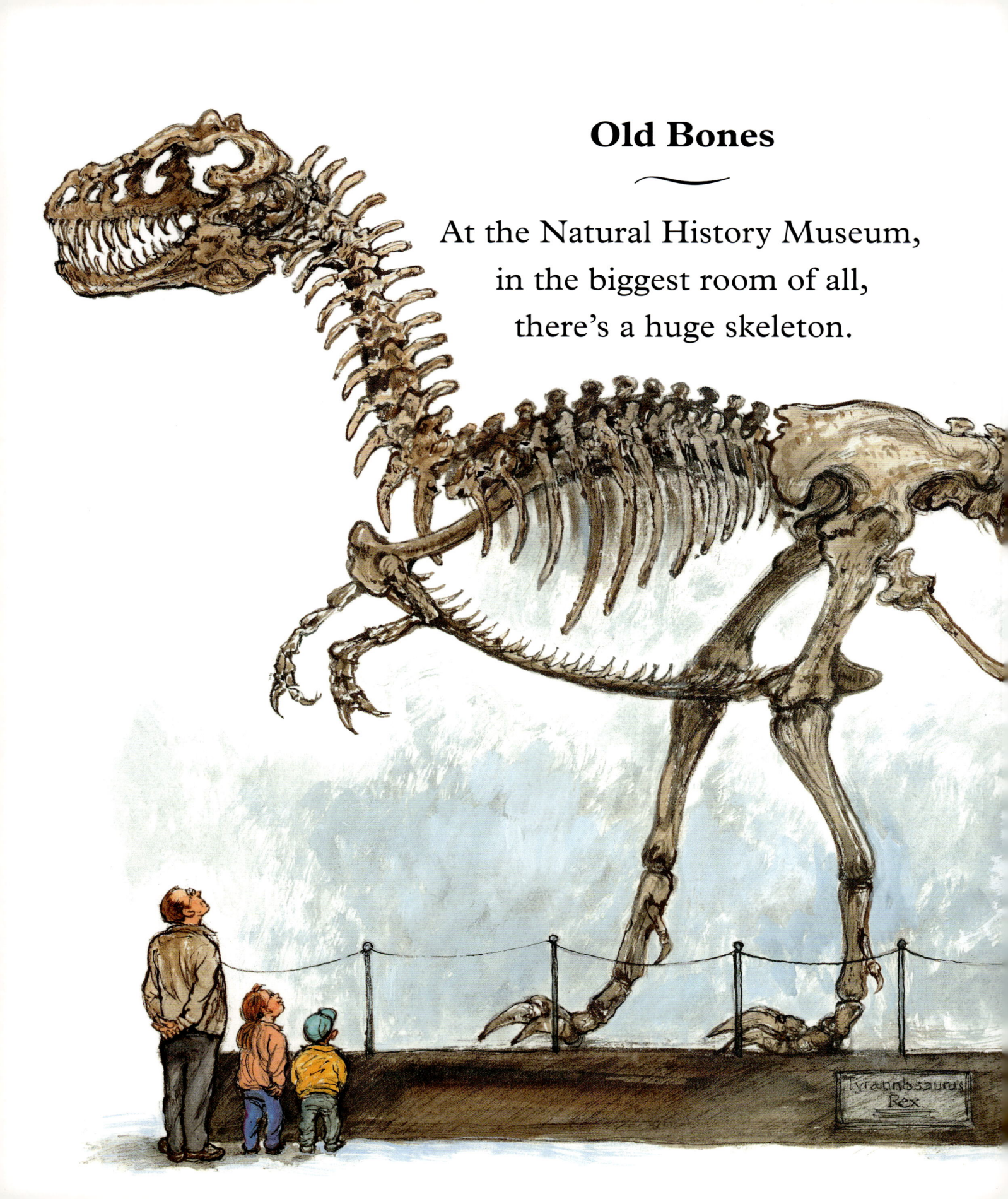

At the Natural History Museum,
in the biggest room of all,
there's a huge skeleton.

It is of an animal who lived long ago, as big as a ship
from head to tail, with a great arched neck
and holes where once there were eyes.

And when Olly and Katie are standing
under its tail, looking at its
great teeth, they wonder
what it would be like
to meet an alive one.

But Dad says there
were no people
living in the world then.

Luckily.

Our Cat Ginger

No cat is as nice as Olly and Katie's cat Ginger. There's the sleek black cat with pale green eyes that they often talk to on their way to the park, and there's the big striped Daddy cat who lives next door. There are four little kittens at their friend Norah's house. And there's Grandma's beautiful Queenie. But no cat – *no* cat – is as nice as Olly and Katie's cat Ginger.

My Friend Betty

There's a place in the park where the farm animals live: the pig with a house of his own, and the hens and geese. But whenever Olly and Katie go there, Katie alway visits Betty the sheep first. She has a nice fat back.

And when she sees Katie she always turns her head and lets her touch her nose. Olly likes rabbits. When they come out of their hutch Olly and Katie are allowed to stroke them – the beautiful black one, the brown ones with silky ears and the white one with pink eyes. But Betty is Katie's special friend.

Hiding

You can't see me, I'm hiding! Here I am.
I'm hiding again! Bet you can't find me this time!
Under a bush in the garden is a very good place
to hide. So is a big umbrella, or down at the end
of the bed. Sometimes Dad hides behind a

newspaper. And Mum hides behind a book on the sofa. You can even hide under a hat. Tortoises hide inside their shells when they aren't feeling friendly. And hamsters hide right at the back of their cages when they want to go to sleep. When the baby hides his eyes he thinks you can't see him. But he's there all the time!

A lot of things seem to hide – the moon behind the clouds and the sun behind the trees. Flowers need to hide in the ground in wintertime. But they come peeping out again in the spring.

Buster always hides when it's time for his bath, and so does Mum's purse when we're all ready to go out shopping.

Our favourite place to hide is behind the kitchen door. Then we jump out – BOO! And can you guess who's hiding behind these curtains?

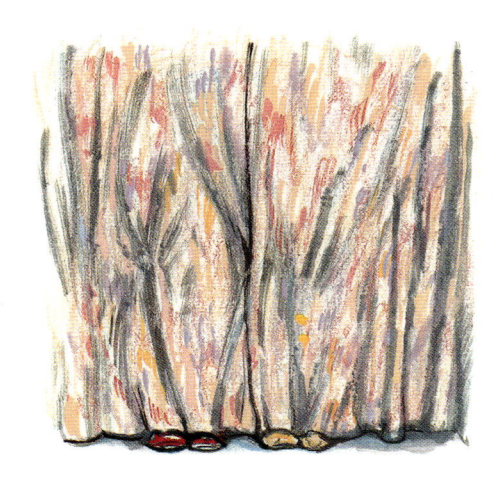

You're right! Now we're coming out – is everyone clapping?

Happy Birthday, Dear Mum

Katie is colouring in a beautiful card for Mum. Because tomorrow, when she wakes up, it will be her birthday! Katie has tried to explain to Olly about birthdays but he doesn't quite understand. He can't remember his own, but he's hoping for balloons. They are his favourite thing at the moment.

Katie has a present for Mum which Dad and Katie bought together. It's a keyring with a sheep on it, so she won't have to search for her keys so often.

They've got a surprise cake with candles. (But not one for every year because Dad says that grown-ups don't always have that.)

Tomorrow Mum will have breakfast in bed.
There will be lots of crushy hugs.
And presents.

Giving

I gave Mum a present on her birthday, all wrapped up in pretty paper. And she gave me a big kiss. I gave Dad a very special picture which I painted at play-group. And he gave me a ride on his shoulders most of the way home.

I gave the baby some slices of my apple. We ate them sitting under the table. At teatime the baby gave me two of his soggy crusts. *That* wasn't much of a present!

You can give someone a cross look or a big smile! You can give a tea party or a seat on a crowded bus.

On my birthday Grandma and Grandpa gave me a beautiful doll's pram. I said "Thank you" and gave them each a big hug.

And I gave my dear Bemily a ride in it, all the way down the garden path and back again.

I tried to give the cat a ride too, but she gave me a nasty scratch!

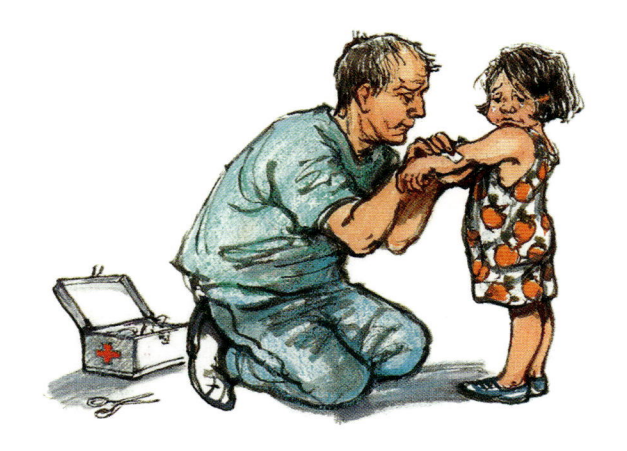

So Dad had to give my poor arm a kiss and a wash and a piece of sticking plaster.

Sometimes, just when I've built a big
castle out of bricks …

the baby comes along and gives it a big swipe!
And it all falls down. Then I feel like giving
the baby a big swipe too.

But I don't, because he *is* my baby brother,
after all.

Chatting

I like chatting. I chat to the cat, and I chat in the car. I chat with friends in the park, and to the lady at the supermarket.

Grown-ups like chatting too. Sometimes these chats go on for rather a long time. The lady next door is an especially good chatter.

When Mum is busy she says that there are just too many chatterboxes around. So I go off and chat to Bemily – but she never says a word. The baby likes a chat on his toy telephone. He makes a lot of calls. But I can chat to Grandma and Grandpa on the real telephone.

Some of the best chats of all are with Dad, when he comes to say good night.

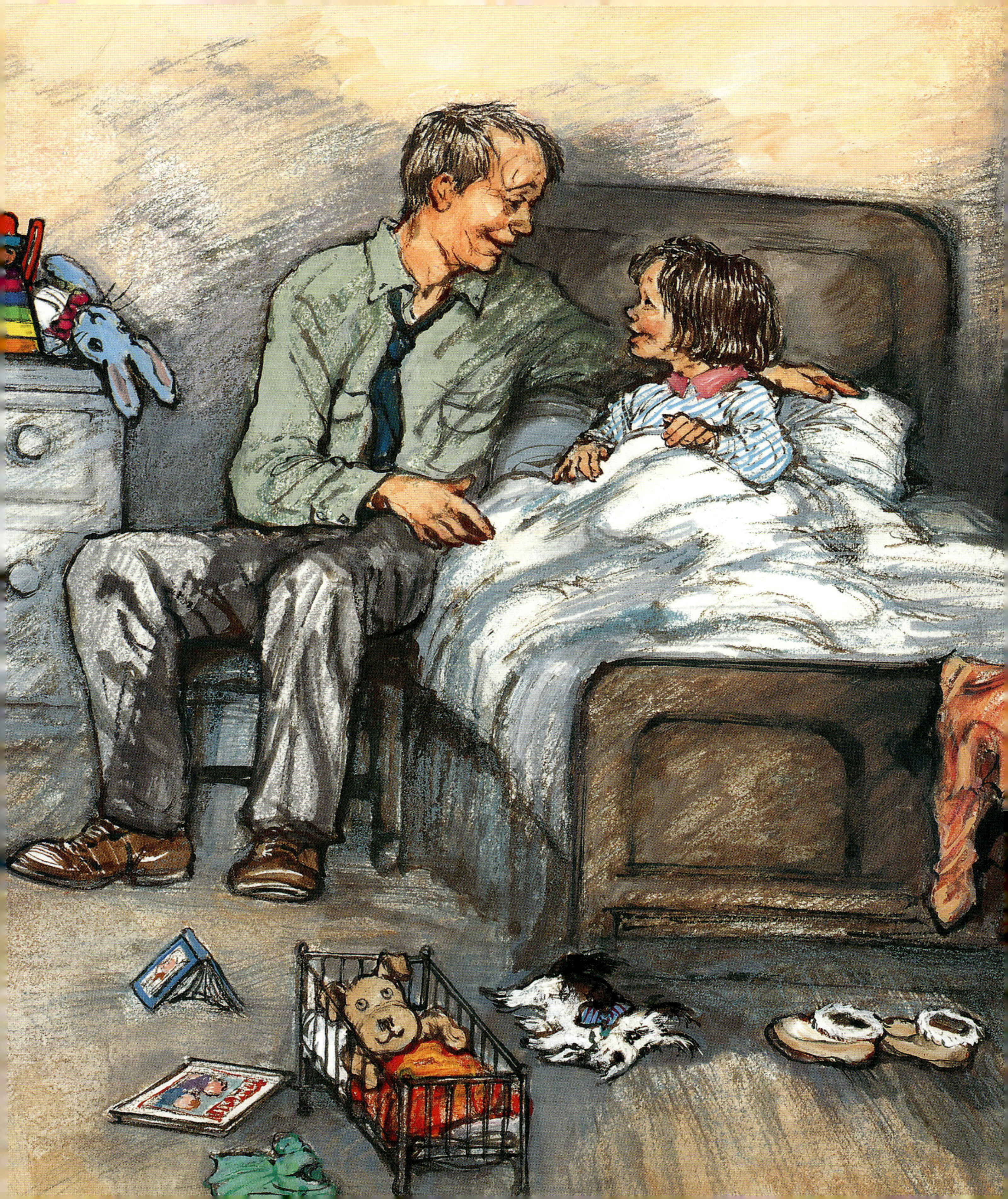

Longer Stories

Wheels

Spring at last! The Easter holidays had arrived and the wheels were out on Trotter Street. Sanjit Lal zipped along on his roller-skates, wearing a smart crash-helmet. Little Pete Patterson rode his red tricycle, ring-a-ding-dinging the bell to let everyone know he was coming.

Harvey and Barney took turns on Barney's skateboard and Mae pushed her baby sister Holly in a brand-new buggy. Some of the big girls and boys had wonderful, new full-size bikes, even racers! They gathered at the corner to show them off. Carlos and Billy had their old bikes.

Billy's mum looked after Carlos in the school holidays, while *his* mum was at work. When she took Billy's baby brother to the park in the afternoon, Carlos and Billy came too and brought their bikes. They were not old enough to ride on the road, of course. It was too dangerous.

The park was the best place to ride. There was a smooth, wide path which went round the play area then into a steep slope. You could whizz down it, cornering at high speed, and free-wheel the rest of the way, past the old band-stand until, braking gently, you ended up at the bottom by the lake where the ducks swam.

The little kids playing and the mums chatting on the benches and the old lady who came to feed the birds all stopped what they were doing and stared as Carlos and Billy flew past.

Whooosh!

There was a narrow, humpbacked bridge over the lake. Carlos and Billy thought it was exciting to race their bikes up one side and down the other. Sometimes Carlos won and sometimes Billy. But if Mr Low, the park-keeper, saw them, he soon put a stop to it. He was very strict about people behaving well in his park. Mr Low did not seem to like fast riding at all, not even on the paths.

Orville, his assistant, was not quite so strict. Sometimes, when Mr Low went off to have a cup of tea in his hut, Orville would call out encouraging things to Carlos and Billy as they raced by.

All the same, Carlos and Billy both wished they had better bikes.

"You can get up a lot more speed on a big bike," said Billy. "They have gears too."

"I've seen one I like in a shop," said Carlos. "Blue and silver with a pump to match."

"I'm going to ask for a new bike for my birthday," said Billy. "It's very soon now."

"It's my birthday soon as well," said Carlos, "and I'm going to get a new bike too."

Carlos asked his mum about this. He had asked her before and he asked her again that evening. But his mum said that new bikes were very expensive. She explained that it was difficult for her to save up for things like bikes. She worked in a bakery and often brought home nice fruit cake and cream buns for Carlos and his big brother Marco – but not very much money.

"Marco's got a proper bike," moaned Carlos.

"He's older than you," said Mum, "and he needs it for his Saturday job. He's saving up for a mountain-bike. When you're bigger, you can learn to ride his old one."

"But I need a new bike *now*," Carlos said.

Mum only answered: "We'll have to see…"

On the afternoon of his birthday, Billy proudly brought his brand-new bike to the park. It was orange, with shiny silver handlebars. Everyone gathered round to admire it. Even Orville left his work to come and have a look.

"Race you!" Billy called out to Carlos, as he pulled away and glided off down the path.

It was not much of a race. Billy won easily. Carlos felt silly pedalling furiously behind, crouched over the handlebars of his old bike. His legs felt too long and his knees kept getting in the way.

After a while, Billy's mum suggested that Billy should give Carlos a turn on his new bike, which he very kindly did.

But when Carlos had swooped down the hill like a bird once or twice, he had to give the beautiful bike back to Billy.

In the end, Carlos gave up wanting to race. There was no point. He threw down his old bike by the lake and sat by himself, tossing pebbles into the water.

He felt cross with Billy. He even felt cross with the ducks who came swimming over to see if he said any bread.

"You wait! You wait till it's my birthday!" he told them.

On the evening of his birthday, Carlos kept wondering if Mum had managed to get him a bike. He thought she could have hidden one in the shed behind their block of flats.

He even secretly slipped out and tried the shed door, but it was locked. Was there a bike inside? He looked through the crack, but he couldn't see anything.

Mum had promised that tomorrow she would bring home a very special cake from the shop – a birthday cake for Carlos! She said that he could ask Billy round for tea. But Carlos didn't want Billy to come to his birthday tea.

In bed that night, Carlos was too excited to sleep.

He kept imagining getting a new bike: a big bike, a blue and silver bike, a bike that was even better and faster than Billy's, which he could show off in the park. He crept to the window and looked down at the shed. There was a light on in there! He could see it shining up through the skylight in the roof. He watched for a long time. Then he went back to bed.

In the morning, Mum gave Carlos a big birthday hug. Marco had gone off early, but he had left a card on the kitchen table with some bears in a spaceship and "Happy Birthday, Carlos" written inside it. There were some parcels on the table too, all wrapped in fancy paper.

"Aren't you going to open them?" asked Mum, beaming.

Carlos pulled off the papers one by one. There was a jigsaw puzzle, a new jacket in dazzling red and green, just like the ones the big boy bikers wore, and a toy car with remote control. Carlos had wanted one ever since he had seen them in a shop and he was very pleased. But he knew at once there was no new bike.

"Marco's going to give you his present when he comes in at teatime," Mum told him.

Carlos knew that Marco's present could not possibly be a new bike. He would not have nearly enough money for that. Inside, Carlos could not help feeling bitterly disappointed.

When Mum asked him if he would like to go and play with Billy that morning and show him his new things, Carlos said no – he would rather go to the shop with Mum. So he took his new car and played with it in the back of the bakery while his mum served the customers. The car went very well. Everyone made a great fuss of Carlos when they heard it was his birthday. One lady bought him a chocolate cream cake and another gave him some money for his piggy-bank.

When they got home, Mum opened a box and brought out a truly wonderful cake. It was pink and white and covered in icing shells and swirls, with silver holders for the candles. There was a plate of fancy pastries too, and ice-cream. Carlos ate a lot of everything. But when the time came to light his candles, he missed having Billy to help him blow them out.

Then Marco walked in. He got hold of Carlos and swung him round, singing "Happy Birthday to you!" Then he ate a very large slice of cake.

"Want to find out what I got for you?" said Marco. "Follow me."

Carlos followed Marco downstairs. All the way down, Carlos was wondering what Marco was going to give him.

He knew it could not be a bike. So what was it? They walked right past the shed. Then at last Carlos saw his present!

It was a go-cart! A real go-cart! It had proper steering and rubber wheels and a seat, and it was painted bright red. Marco had made it himself.

Carlos was too surprised to speak. Never, ever, in his wildest dreams had he imagined owning a go-cart! He looked at it for a long time. He stroked its wheels and its little seat. Then he put his head against Marco's arm.

"Thanks, Marco," he said.

It was the last day of the holidays. Most of Trotter Street had turned up in the park for the big event: the Non-Bicycle Race! The starters were already lined up – Sanjit, Sam and Ruby Roberts were on roller-skates; Harvey and Barney had skateboards. Jim Zolinski and Brains Barrington were in their box-on-wheels; Frankie had borrowed a scooter, and Mae and Debbie had one roller-skate each. Carlos was at the controls of his new go-cart, with Billy crouching behind him. Now Josie lifted the starter's flag…

Ready, steady, GO! Cheering mums, dads and toddlers lined the track. The Bird Lady was there and Orville too. Even Mr Low popped his head round the door of his hut to watch, though mostly to keep an eye on his flower-beds.

Past the play area, into the steep slope, gaining speed then cornering wildly, sometimes crashing but managing to scramble on again, weaving, coasting, trundling they went – all the way down to the lake.

And who came first?
Carlos and Billy in
the wonderful go-cart,
of course!

The Big Concrete Lorry

The Patterson family lived at number twenty-six Trotter Street. There was Mum, Dad, Josie, Harvey and little Pete. Also Murdoch, their dog.

Their house had a patch of garden at the back with a flower-bed, a washing line and an apple tree. In front there was only just room between the house and the street for some flower-pots and a couple of dustbins.

Josie had a room of her own. It was jam-packed with *her* things.

Harvey and little Pete shared the back bedroom. It was jam-packed with *their* things.

Murdoch had a basket in the kitchen. But often (though he wasn't supposed to) he slept at the bottom of Harvey's bed. Murdoch was a roly-poly dog who fitted nicely under Harvey's feet, like a plump hot-water bottle.

The Pattersons' hall was full of coats, boots, skateboards and buggies. The family living room was very often full of Pattersons. Sometimes – when Josie was doing her homework at one end of the table and Mum was cutting out a blouse at the other end, and Dad was eating his supper in front of the television, and little Pete was playing with his toy cars, and Harvey and Murdoch were flopping about all over the sofa – it seemed as though the room was so full, it would burst!

"We must have more space!" moaned Mum.

"We could move to a bigger house," said Dad, "if only big houses weren't so expensive."

All the family said that they couldn't possibly move to a new house. They loved Trotter Street far too much.

Then Dad had a good idea. "We could build an extension!" he cried.

Harvey wanted to know what an extension was. Dad explained that it was an extra room at the back, just like the one which Mr Lal has built next door. Mr Lal's extension was full of beautiful pot-plants and ornaments.

All the Pattersons thought that to have an extension like Mr Lal's would be a very good idea. So Dad brought home some brochures showing pictures of splendid extensions with happy people looking out of them.

"I'll put it up myself!" said Dad.

"Are you sure you can manage it?" Mum asked anxiously.

Dad said that Mr Lal and his son Rhajit, and Frankie and Mae's dad from up the street, had promised to help him, so it would be all right.

Next week, a delivery van drew up outside the Pattersons' house and some men unloaded bits of wood and windows and doors and stacked them in the back garden. This was the extension, all in pieces.

"Now we need some bricks," said Dad.

A few days later another truck arrived. It had "JIFFY BUILDING CO" written on it and, underneath, "Joe and Jimmy Best".

"Load of bricks you ordered!" said jolly Joe Best, jumping from the cab.

Then he and Jimmy lowered the flap at the back of the truck and began unloading the bricks. They took them through the house and stacked them in the garden.

After they had driven off, Harvey, Josie and little Pete had a great time playing on the bricks, while Mum vacuumed away the dirty footprints left by Joe and Jimmy.

The following morning, Dad got up very early and put on his old trousers, saying that he was going to dig a foundation.

Of course, Harvey wanted to know what a foundation was. Dad explained that it was a solid base for the extension walls to stand on.

Mr Lal came round after breakfast and helped Dad measure the space for the extension. They marked it out carefully with string, pegged to the ground. Then Dad, Mr Lal and Rhajit, and Frankie and Mae's dad began to dig a trench following the line of the string.

Little Pete thought all this was very interesting. He fetched his spade and began to dig too. So did Murdoch.

When the trench was finished, the men cleared the space where the floor was to be, put down bits of brick and rubble and covered them with a plastic sheet. Now everything was ready for the concrete. But first, an Inspector came to look at it, to make sure it had all been done properly.

Meanwhile, Josie and Harvey pretended that the extension was already built and they were having lunch inside. Josie imagined that it had pink wallpaper and Harvey imagined that there were curtains with a pattern of aeroplanes.

Dad was so tired the next day that he didn't get up early. Mum took him a cup of tea in bed. While the rest of the family were having breakfast, they heard a great noise in the street.

They all hurried outside. A lorry had arrived at their house. It was huge! It had a big drum that turned slowly round and round – CRRURK, CRRURK, CRRURK! On the side of the lorry was written, "JIFFY READY-MIX CONCRETE CO".

Out jumped jolly Joe Best. "Load of concrete you ordered!" he called cheerfully.

"Not this morning, surely?" said Mum. "I'm sure we didn't..."

But it was too late. Jimmy had already pulled a lever and the big drum poured out a load of concrete, all in a rush. *Slop! Slurp! Dollop! Splosh!* Just like that! It landed in a shivering heap right outside the Pattersons' front door.

Dad rushed downstairs, pulling on his trousers over his pyjamas.

"We weren't expecting you today!" he shouted.

"That's okay. Just sign here," said Joe. Then he leapt back into his seat. "It's quick-setting!" he called from the cab window. "Be hard as a rock in a couple of hours. Better get busy!"

"But we haven't..." Dad called back.

But Jimmy was already revving up the engine. The big concrete lorry roared away in a cloud of dust.

"Quick!" cried Dad, picking up a shovel.
"Quick!" shrieked Mum, searching for a spade.
"Grab those buckets!"
"Fetch the wheelbarrow!"
"Run for the neighbours!"
"*The quick-setting concrete is soon going to set!*"

Never had the Pattersons moved so fast. Mum began to shovel up the concrete into the wheelbarrow and trundle it through the house, while Dad shovelled and smoothed it down over the foundation at the back.

Josie and Harvey ran to fetch Mr Lal and Rhajit from next door, and Frankie and Mae's dad from up the street.
And they all came running.
The neighbours pitched in and shovelled and spread too.

Josie, Harvey and little Pete ran up and down with buckets. Murdoch joined in, barking loudly.

Everyone laboured and struggled and fell over one another's feet. They shovelled and heaved and trundled concrete from the front of the house to the back. And steadily the heap on the pavement grew smaller and smaller.

"Quick! It's beginning to set!" shouted Mum.

Everyone worked faster and faster.

"Done at last!" gasped Dad, throwing down his shovel and wiping his hands on his trousers.

Then all the workers rested. The foundation was finished. Only a small hill of concrete was left beside the front door. It had set so hard that nothing in the world would shift it.

The extension went up bit by bit. First, a low brick wall, then the roof, windows and door.

And at last the Patterson family were able to move in.

They were so pleased with their beautiful new extension that they gave a party for all their neighbours.

Harvey and little Pete were extra pleased with the small concrete hill which stood outside their front door. None of their friends had one like it. It was great for sitting on and for racing toy cars down.

And if you ever climbed up and stood on the top, you could see right to the very end of Trotter Street.

LEARNING

ABC

Aa

is for aeroplane

High in the sky, an aeroplane zooms by.
Olly and I wonder how far away it is going.

Bb

is for bouncing ball!
When I throw my big shiny
ball it bounces away from me ...
bounce, bounce, bounce.

Cc

is for cat

Our cat is called Ginger. No cat is as nice as she is.

Dd

is for Dad who is very good at cooking ... and for our dog, Buster, who always wants to join in with everything we are doing.

Ee

is for everyone

This is my family:
Mum, Dad, Olly
and me.

Ff

is for farm animals

There is a place in the park where we go
and see them up close.

Gg

is for Grandma and Grandpa

They are very special.
They often come to visit and look after us sometimes when Mum and Dad are busy.

Hh is for hats

We have some great hats in our dressing up box. Olly likes to try them on, even if they are too big for him.

Ii

is for ice cream

Grandpa always treats me to an ice cream when we go to the park together.

Jj

is for jam and jar

When we've finished a jar of jam we can use it for water to wash our paintbrushes and keep our colours clean.

Kk

is for Katie – that's me!

And this is my little brother Olly.

Ll

is for leaves

In the autumn they turn all kinds of beautiful colours and you can wade through them when they fall from the trees.

Mm

is for Mum

I love having a cuddle with Mum at the end of the day when she reads my bedtime story.

Nn

is for noise

Olly and I can make lots of noise, especially when I am dancing and singing and he joins in with a saucepan and spoon.

Oo

is for Olly, of course!

He can be annoying
sometimes, but he loves it when we spend
time together and we play some great games.

Pp

is for play-group

I have lots of fun at play-group with my friends.

Qq

is for queen

At Christmas, I got a crown in my cracker and pretended to be a queen.

Rr

is for rainbow

Sometimes, when it's sunny and rainy at the same time, you can see a beautiful arc of colours in the sky.

Ss is for stories

Olly and I love going to the library on Saturday afternoons to listen to stories.

Tt is for toys

My favourite toy is called Bemily. She is not quite a hippo and not quite a bear and I take her with me wherever I go.

Uu

is for umbrella

Olly and I have found a really good place to hide.

Vv

is for vacuum cleaner

It vroom-vroom-vrooms when Dad cleans the carpet.

Ww is for wellies

Olly and I need our wellies when we go out and splash in puddles.

Xx
is for kisses

Mum gave me an extra-special kiss when I gave her a birthday present all wrapped up in pretty paper.

Yy
is for yellow

Yellow is the colour of sunshine, and custard, and my favourite summery dress.

Zz is for zzzzz

Now it's sleepytime.

Good night, everyone!

1.

One is me, Katie.
Here I am,
all by myself.

2

But I'm not by myself for long.
Here comes Olly, my baby brother,
and that makes **two** of us.

2

You need **two**
to play a game
of hide and seek.

Two things often go together
in pairs, like shoes and socks …

or these twin babies who
were born on the very
same day.

3 •••

Three is company
when my friend Norah
comes to play …

3 ...

or when our cat
Ginger is in a good
mood and lets us stroke her.

4 ••••

My friend Norah's cat
has **four** dear little kittens.
Each of them has **four** neat
white paws.

4 ● ● ● ●

There are **four** people in our family. When we go out we usually take our dog Buster too and that makes **five**. Buster likes to chase birds, but he never catches any.

5 ●●●●●

Five fingers on each hand are very useful for counting.

And here are **five** falling leaves…

5

Five of us do ballet together:
Amanda and James and Kim and
Norah and me.

But when Olly tries to join in, there are **six**.

6 ●●●●●

There are **six** of us when Grandma and Grandpa come to visit.

And when I give my own special tea party in the garden there are **six** of us too. Buster is allowed to come as long as he doesn't try to lick the plates.

7 ●●●●●●●

Here are:

seven side by side dancers …

seven swift runners …

and **seven** stylish hats.

8 • • • • • • • •

And here are **eight** busy bouncers.

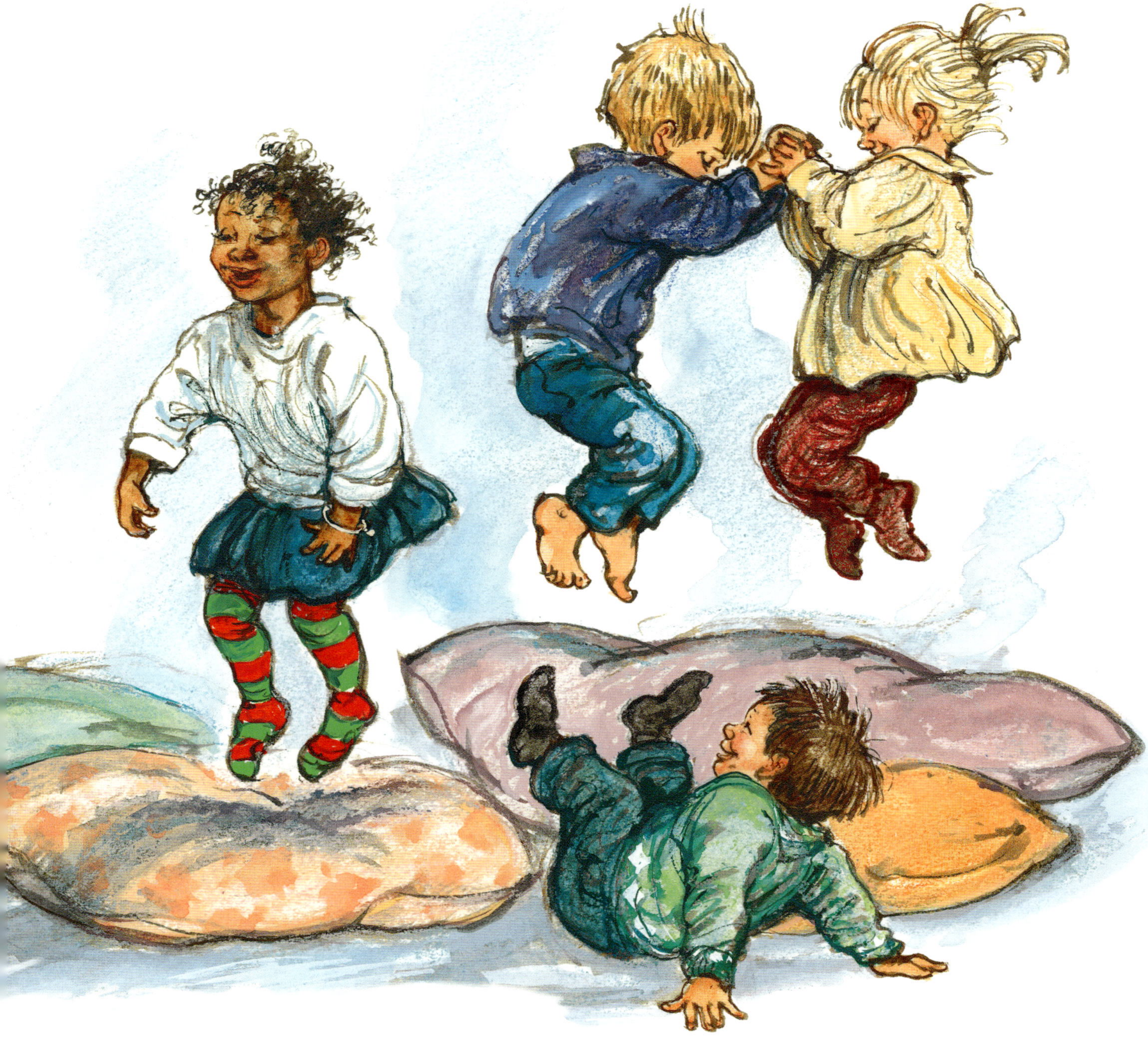

9 ●●●●●●●●●

Eight children and one big brown dog make **nine**.

Is the **ninth** brick going to make my tower fall down?

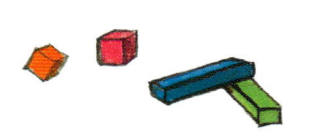

Yes! But never mind!

10

Ten people on a crowded bus. But hooray! Here's one kind gentleman giving us his seat.

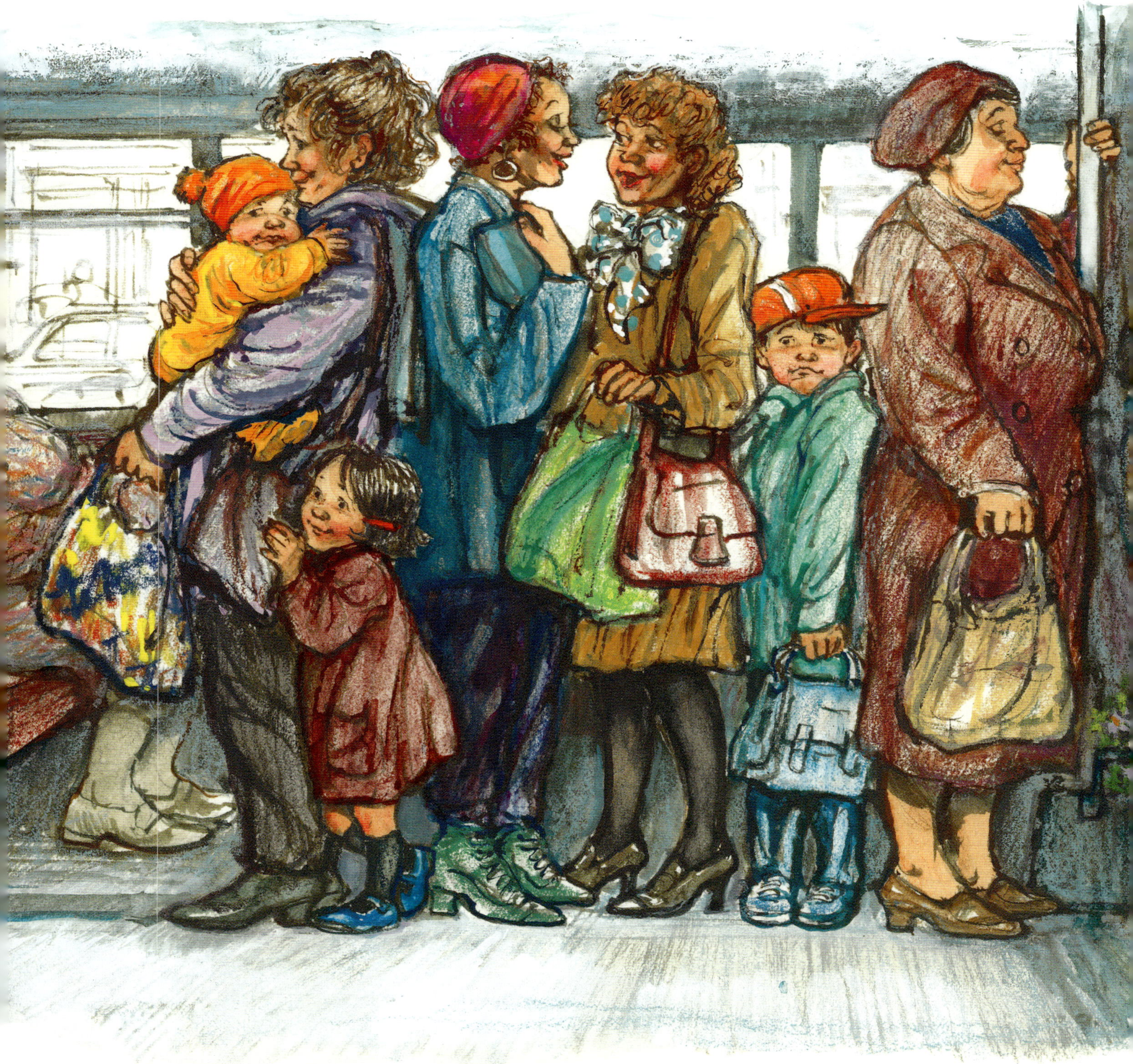

Some things are too many to count –
like blossoms falling from a tree
or raindrops into a puddle …
or flowers in the springtime

or clouds in the sky
going up and up…
Numbers go on
forever.

Colours

blue

Baby blues,
navy blues,
blue socks,
blue shoes,

Blue plate, blue mug,
blue flowers in a
blue jug.

And fluffy white clouds floating by

In a great big beautiful bright blue sky.

yellow

Syrup dripping from a spoon,

Buttercups,

A harvest moon.

Sun like honey on the floor,

Warm as the steps by our back door.

red

Rosy apples, dark cherries,
Scarlet leaves, bright berries.

And when the winter's day is done,
A fiery sky, a big red sun.

Red and yellow make
orange

Tangerines and apricots,
Orange flowers in orange pots.

Orange glow on an orange mat,
Marmalade toast and a marmalade cat.

Blue and red make

purple

Berries in the bramble patch.
Pick them (but mind the thorns don't scratch)!

Purple blossom, pale and dark,
Spreading with springtime in the park.

Blue and yellow make

green

Grasshoppers, greenflies, gooseberries, cat's eyes.

Green lettuce, green peas
Green shade from green trees.
And grass as far as you can see
Like green waves in a green sea.

black

Shiny boots, a witch's hat.

Black cloak, black cat.

Black crows cawing high,

Winter trees against the sky.

white

Thistledown like white fluff,
Dandelion clocks to puff.
White cover on my bed,
White pillow for my head.

White snowflakes, whirling down,
Covering gardens, roofs and towns.

All Shapes and Sizes

Boxes have flat sides,
Balls are round.
High is far up in the sky,
Low is near the ground.

Some of us are rather short,
Some are tall.

Some pets are large,

Some are small.

Our cat's very fat,
Next door's is thin.

Big Teddy's out,
Little Teddy's in.

Squeeze through narrow spaces,

Run through wide,

Climb up the ladder,

Slip down the slide.

Get behind to push,

Get in front to pull.

This jar's empty,

Now it's full.

Hats can be many sizes,

So can feet,

Children of all ages
playing in the street.

We can stand up
very straight,

or we can bend.

Here's a
beginning,

and this is
the end!